Application of NLP in Environmental Behavior Change Encouraging Sustainable Choices

By Rex Morton

Copyright Page

Disclaimer

This book is intended to provide information about the fields of Neuro-Linguistic Programming (NLP) and Cognitive Behavioural Therapy (CBT) and their potential integration. While the author has made every effort to ensure that the information was correct at the time of publication, the author does not assume and hereby disclaims any liability to any party for any loss, damage, or disruption caused by errors or omissions, whether such errors or omissions result from negligence, accident, or any other cause.

The contents of this book should not be used as a substitute for professional advice, diagnosis, or treatment. The reader should always consult with a qualified healthcare provider about any mental health concerns or conditions. Never disregard professional psychological or medical advice or delay in seeking it because of something you have read in this book.

The views expressed in this work are solely those of the author and do not necessarily reflect the views of the publisher, and the publisher hereby disclaims any responsibility for them.

The inclusion of websites, links, or references to other resources does not mean that the author or the publisher endorses the information the organization or website may provide or recommendations it might make. Furthermore, the author does not guarantee the accuracy of the information these resources provide.

The use of any information provided in this book is solely at your own risk.

Chapter 1: Introduction

Welcome to the nexus of neuro-linguistic programming (NLP) and environmental behavior change, a field of study that is as intriguing as it is promising in fostering sustainable choices. As you embark on this journey, you will encounter innovative perspectives on the application of NLP to change attitudes, beliefs, and behaviors concerning our environment and the choices we make on a daily basis.

This book, "Application of Neuro-Linguistic Programming in Environmental Behavior Change: Encouraging Sustainable Choices," provides a comprehensive exploration of how NLP, a method of influencing brain behavior through the use of language and other types of communication, can help drive significant and positive changes in environmental behavior. It presents a blend of theoretical concepts, practical applications, and relevant case studies to understand and implement this powerful tool in the sphere of environmental sustainability.

The importance and relevance of this topic are more pronounced than ever before. As our planet grapples with climate change, deforestation, loss of biodiversity, water scarcity, pollution, and myriad other environmental issues, it has become essential to alter our behaviors and attitudes towards our environment. Despite many initiatives and awareness campaigns, achieving substantive change in environmental behavior remains a challenge. This is where the techniques of NLP can be transformative. It can help break down cognitive barriers, change perspectives, and encourage sustainable choices, thus leading us towards a more sustainable future.

The objectives of this book are multifaceted:

Understanding NLP: To delve deep into the fundamentals of NLP – its history, principles, and various techniques. A thorough understanding of NLP forms the foundation for its application in any field, including environmental behavior change.

Exploring Environmental Behavior: To analyze the nature of environmental behavior and understand its psychological underpinnings. We will also study how this behavior can be influenced by various factors.

Linking NLP and Environmental Behavior: To investigate the connection between NLP and behavior change, particularly focusing on environmental behavior. We will also present case studies where NLP has been successfully applied to change behavior.

Applying NLP Techniques for Sustainability: To present specific NLP techniques that can encourage sustainable choices, and illustrate their application through real-world examples.

Highlighting the Role of NLP in Environmental Education and Communication: To discuss how NLP can be incorporated into environmental education and communication strategies to increase their effectiveness.

Overcoming Barriers: To address the common obstacles to environmental behavior change and how NLP can be utilized to overcome these challenges.

Discussing Ethical Considerations and Limitations: Finally, to address the ethical considerations and potential limitations in applying NLP for behavior change and discuss how these can be mitigated.

In writing this book, my goal is to provide you with a holistic understanding of the subject matter, along with practical knowledge that you can apply in your own spheres of influence to encourage sustainable choices. The journey ahead is fascinating and holds the promise of substantial progress in the field of environmental sustainability. We hope you find this exploration both enlightening and empowering.

Chapter 2: Understanding Neuro-Linguistic Programming (NLP)

Neuro-Linguistic Programming, better known as NLP, is a complex and innovative approach to understanding human cognition, communication, and behavior. To harness its power in altering environmental behavior, we first need to comprehend its origin, fundamental principles, and the diverse techniques it offers.

The History of NLP

NLP was developed in the mid-1970s by Richard Bandler, a psychology student, and John Grinder, a linguistics professor. Bandler and Grinder aimed to identify and replicate the patterns of thought and behavior that led to success. They studied three leading therapists of the time - Fritz Perls, Virginia Satir, and Milton Erickson - and outlined their effective strategies, techniques, and language patterns, thus giving birth to the core methodologies of NLP.

Over the years, NLP evolved, encompassing numerous models and strategies, becoming an influential tool in therapy, coaching, education, business, and personal development.

Fundamental Principles of NLP

NLP operates based on several foundational principles, which are integral to understanding its application:

The Map is Not the Territory: This principle suggests that our perception of reality is not reality itself, but merely a mental map that we've constructed. Therefore, by changing this map, we can alter our reality.

There is No Failure, Only Feedback: NLP promotes a positive outlook towards challenges and setbacks, viewing them as opportunities for learning and improvement.

The Mind and Body are Part of the Same System: This implies that our thoughts, emotions, and physical state are interconnected. A change in one can influence the others.

People Have All the Resources They Need to Succeed: NLP assumes that everyone has the necessary resources within them to effect positive change. They just need to discover and mobilize these resources.

If One Person Can Do Something, Anyone Can Learn to Do It: This principle, central to NLP's origins, is the belief that successful strategies can be modeled and taught to others.

Techniques and Strategies in NLP

Several techniques underpin NLP, each serving a unique purpose. Some of these include:

Rapport: Building rapport involves creating a sense of trust and understanding, which is essential for effective communication and influence. NLP practitioners often use mirroring and matching techniques to establish rapport.

Anchoring: Anchoring is the process of associating a specific physical touch, sight, or sound with a particular state of mind or emotion, enabling the individual to recall this state at will.

Swish Patterns: This technique is used to change undesired habits or behaviors. It involves replacing the mental image associated with the unwanted behavior with the image of the desired outcome.

Reframing: Reframing is about changing the way we perceive an event, thus changing its meaning and our response to it. This technique is particularly useful in altering limiting beliefs or negative emotions associated with an event.

Meta Model: The Meta Model is a set of language patterns that help uncover the deeper meaning in communication, thereby providing clarity and overcoming misunderstandings.

Milton Model: Named after the famed therapist Milton Erickson, this model uses vague and metaphorical language to induce a trance-like state and facilitate change at the subconscious level.

Strategy Elicitation: This NLP technique is used to uncover the mental strategies an individual uses for decision-making, learning, motivation, and other cognitive processes. Once known, these strategies can be modified or enhanced.

Understanding these principles and techniques provides a strong foundation for harnessing NLP's potential to shape environmental behavior. As we delve deeper into this subject in the upcoming chapters, you will get a chance to see these principles and techniques in action, encouraging sustainable choices and behaviors.

As we dive deeper into our exploration of applying Neuro-Linguistic Programming (NLP) in encouraging sustainable choices, it's essential to understand the concept of environmental behavior: what it is, why it matters, the factors that influence it, and the psychology underpinning it.

Understanding Environmental Behavior: What it is and Why it Matters

Environmental behavior, in its broadest sense, refers to the actions and practices undertaken by individuals, communities, or organizations that impact the environment. This includes everything from daily habits like recycling, conserving water, and reducing energy consumption to larger decisions such as supporting clean energy sources, choosing environmentally-friendly products, or advocating for policies that protect the environment.

The importance of environmental behavior cannot be overstated. The collective behavior of human beings has a profound impact on our planet. Our consumption patterns, energy use, waste generation, and countless other behaviors contribute to environmental issues such as pollution, climate change, deforestation, and loss of biodiversity. Modifying environmental behavior, therefore, is crucial in addressing these challenges and paving the way for a sustainable future.

Factors Influencing Environmental Behavior

Environmental behavior is complex, shaped by an interplay of multiple factors:

Knowledge and Awareness: Understanding environmental issues is often the first step towards adopting sustainable behaviors. Education and awareness campaigns play a significant role in shaping environmental behavior.

Attitudes and Beliefs: People's attitudes towards the environment, their beliefs about their ability to make a difference, and their values concerning nature significantly influence their environmental behavior.

Social Influences: Social norms, peer pressure, and cultural practices also shape environmental behavior. People are more likely to adopt sustainable behaviors if they perceive them as socially acceptable or desirable.

Economic Factors: Costs and benefits associated with behaviors influence choices. If environmentally-friendly options are costlier or less convenient, people may be less likely to choose them.

Political and Institutional Factors: Laws, regulations, and institutional policies can drive environmental behavior by incentivizing sustainable practices or penalizing harmful ones.

Physical Context: The physical environment, including infrastructure and accessibility of resources, can facilitate or impede sustainable behaviors.

The Psychology Behind Environmental Behavior

Psychology provides insights into why people behave the way they do towards the environment. Some key psychological constructs relevant to environmental behavior include:

Environmental Attitudes: These refer to individuals' evaluative judgments about environmental issues. A positive environmental attitude often, but not always, translates into sustainable behavior.

Perceived Behavioral Control: This refers to individuals' beliefs about their capacity to perform a particular behavior. People who believe they have the resources and opportunities to act sustainably are more likely to do so.

Personal Norms: Personal norms are the moral obligations individuals feel towards engaging in pro-environmental behaviors. A strong personal norm can be a powerful motivator for action.

Environmental Identity: This is the degree to which individuals perceive themselves as being connected with nature. Individuals with a strong environmental identity tend to demonstrate more sustainable behaviors.

Locus of Control: This refers to individuals' beliefs about the control they have over events that affect them. Those with a strong internal locus of control believe that they can influence environmental outcomes and are hence more likely to act sustainably.

Understanding environmental behavior and the factors that influence it is crucial as we explore the application of NLP in this context. In the coming chapters, we will see how we can apply NLP principles and techniques to influence these factors and promote sustainable behaviors.

The transformative power of Neuro-Linguistic Programming (NLP) lies in its ability to alter behavior. Understanding the link between NLP and behavior change is critical in leveraging this tool to influence environmental behavior.

The Application of NLP in Behavior Modification

NLP provides a range of techniques that facilitate behavior modification. NLP's core principle is that an individual's perception of the world, their 'map', influences their actions. By changing this map, NLP can effectively modify behavior.

For instance, NLP techniques such as reframing can help individuals alter their perceptions and feelings about specific behaviors, making them more appealing or less daunting. Similarly, techniques like anchoring can help individuals associate positive feelings with desired behaviors, thereby increasing their likelihood.

Through pattern interruption, NLP can disrupt habitual behaviors, creating room for the introduction of new, desired behaviors. The meta-model can uncover underlying beliefs and assumptions that drive behavior, enabling individuals to challenge and change these limiting beliefs.

Hypothetical Case Studies: Successful Applications of NLP in Behavior Change

NLP has been successfully applied in various fields to bring about behavior change:

In Personal Development: Life coaches often use NLP to help individuals overcome limiting beliefs, fears, or procrastination, encouraging more productive behaviors. For instance, through techniques like swish patterns, individuals have managed to break patterns of procrastination, replacing them with more productive habits.

In Business: Companies use NLP to enhance leadership, improve teamwork, and boost sales performance. For example, by using NLP techniques to improve communication and rapport, leaders have been able to foster better team collaboration.

In Therapy: Therapists have used NLP to help clients change destructive behaviors, like smoking or overeating. Techniques like future pacing (where the client is led to visualize themselves in the future without the undesired behavior) have been particularly effective.

Understanding How NLP Can Influence Environmental Behavior

Given its success in other fields, NLP holds tremendous potential to influence environmental behavior.

Changing Perceptions: By reframing how individuals perceive environmental behaviors, NLP can help make these behaviors more appealing. For instance, instead of viewing recycling as a tedious chore, individuals can be led to see it as a meaningful contribution to preserving the environment.

Breaking Old Habits: NLP techniques can disrupt habitual behaviors that harm the environment, like excessive water or electricity usage, and help form more sustainable habits.

Overcoming Resistance: Many individuals resist adopting sustainable behaviors due to perceived inconvenience or lack of belief in their impact. NLP can help overcome these barriers by altering the underlying beliefs and assumptions.

Fostering a Connection with Nature: Techniques like visualization and anchoring can be used to deepen individuals' connection with nature, thereby motivating more sustainable behaviors.

This chapter has bridged the gap between understanding the principles of NLP and the imminent application in altering environmental behaviors. As we delve further into the subsequent chapters, we will explore specific NLP techniques and how they can be employed to promote sustainable choices.

Neuro-Linguistic Programming's power in shaping behavior can be harnessed to influence perceptions about sustainability and promote environmentally-friendly actions. This chapter focuses on applying NLP techniques like reframing, anchoring, and the swish pattern to environmental behavior, including specific examples and case studies.

How NLP Can Shape Perceptions About Sustainability

Our perception of sustainability and sustainable actions can significantly influence our environmental behaviors. By changing the way we perceive these behaviors, NLP can make them more appealing and less daunting.

For example, using public transportation instead of driving personal cars may be seen by some as inconvenient. However, using NLP's reframing technique, this perception can be changed. The focus could be shifted from 'inconvenience' to the benefits such as reducing carbon emissions, saving money, and the opportunity for productive use of commute time.

Reframing, Anchoring, and Swish Pattern in the Context of Environmental Behavior

1. Reframing: Reframing involves changing the way we perceive an event or behavior, thus changing its meaning and our response to it.

For instance, an individual might view reducing meat consumption as a loss of pleasure (negative frame). An NLP practitioner could help reframe this to focus on the health benefits of a plant-based diet, the ethical advantages of reducing animal cruelty, and the positive environmental impact of lower meat consumption (positive frame).

2. Anchoring: Anchoring is the process of associating a particular state of mind or emotion with a specific stimulus.

A practical example of this could be to associate the feeling of happiness or accomplishment with sustainable actions. For instance, every time someone recycles, they could perform a small action (like a thumbs up or a self-congratulatory phrase) that acts as an anchor, triggering feelings of positivity and thereby reinforcing the behavior.

3. Swish Pattern: This technique is often used to replace an undesired habit with a desirable one. It involves visualizing the unwanted behavior and then quickly 'swishing' it away and replacing it with an image of the desired behavior.

Consider someone who habitually uses disposable plastic bottles for drinking water. Through the Swish Pattern, they would visualize this behavior and then swiftly 'swish' it away and replace it with a vision of themselves using a refillable water bottle, thereby encouraging the adoption of the new, sustainable behavior.

Case Studies: Application of These Techniques in Promoting Sustainability

Several case studies illustrate the successful application of these NLP techniques to promote sustainable behavior:

1. Community-Based Social Marketing (CBSM): Doug McKenzie-Mohr, an environmental psychologist, has been using principles similar to reframing in CBSM campaigns for decades. For instance, in one campaign, instead of urging people to reduce energy consumption to combat climate change—a somewhat abstract concept—participants were encouraged to 'keep your home cozy' by properly insulating it. This reframing around comfort made the behavior change more appealing to many people.

2. The 'Blue Bin' Recycling Program: The City of Toronto used principles akin to anchoring when they introduced their Blue Bin recycling program. They created a direct visual association between the blue bin and recycling, which eventually triggered feelings of civic duty and environmental responsibility, leading to a significant increase in recycling rates.

3. Plastic Bag Consumption in Supermarkets: A supermarket chain conducted an experiment where they used the swish pattern technique to reduce plastic bag usage. Shoppers were shown an image of plastic bag pollution and then 'swished' it to an image of a reusable bag. Posters and media reinforcing this swish pattern were displayed around the store, leading to a measurable decrease in plastic bag requests.

By understanding and applying these NLP techniques, we can potentially instigate a significant shift towards more sustainable behaviors and choices, paving the way for a healthier environment.

Education is a vital tool for sustainable development. As we strive to promote sustainable choices, a key avenue to explore is environmental education, where NLP can play a transformative role.

Importance of Education in Sustainability

Environmental education provides individuals with the knowledge, skills, attitudes, and motivation to make informed decisions and take responsible actions for the protection of the environment.

Education fosters awareness about the environmental implications of our choices, encourages a sense of responsibility, and empowers individuals with the tools to contribute towards sustainable development. By promoting understanding and fostering sustainable habits from a young age, environmental education plays a crucial role in shaping future generations of environmentally conscious citizens.

Use of NLP in Teaching and Learning about Environmental Issues

In the realm of environmental education, NLP can be a powerful tool for enhancing teaching and learning about environmental issues. Here's how:

Creating Engaging Narratives: NLP can help educators craft compelling narratives about environmental issues that appeal to students' emotions, making the content more engaging and memorable.

Enhancing Understanding: By using NLP techniques like metaphors and analogies, complex environmental concepts can be broken down into simpler, more relatable ideas, improving comprehension.

Shaping Attitudes and Beliefs: Techniques like reframing can help shape students' attitudes towards the environment and sustainability, fostering a positive and proactive mindset.

Motivating Action: Through techniques like future pacing, educators can help students visualize the positive outcomes of their sustainable actions, motivating them to put their learning into practice.

Case Studies of Successful Environmental Education Initiatives Using NLP

Several educational initiatives have successfully incorporated NLP techniques to improve environmental education:

Green Schools Program: This initiative utilized NLP techniques to enhance environmental education in schools. They reframed environmental education as not just about learning facts but about being 'planet protectors'. This shift in perspective motivated students to take active roles in environmental conservation, like setting up recycling programs in their schools.

The Climate Reality Project: Founded by Al Gore, this initiative uses compelling narratives and metaphors to make the complex topic of climate change more understandable and emotionally engaging. By training individuals to be Climate Reality Leaders, they create a multiplier effect, spreading climate awareness using NLP principles.

The Energy Detective Program: This energy conservation program reframed energy-saving as a detective game for students. By turning off unnecessary lights and devices in their schools, students could 'solve' energy waste mysteries. This innovative application of NLP techniques made the learning process more enjoyable and encouraged real-world action.

The integration of NLP techniques in environmental education can enhance learning experiences, foster positive attitudes, and motivate sustainable actions. As we look towards a sustainable future, the intersection of NLP and environmental education holds immense potential.

Environmental communication plays a pivotal role in promoting sustainable behavior. How we articulate environmental issues and their relevance can significantly impact public response. Here, Neuro-Linguistic Programming (NLP) provides us with tools for more persuasive, engaging, and impactful communication.

Role of Effective Communication in Promoting Sustainable Behavior

Communication is at the heart of behavior change. Effective communication can heighten awareness, inform understanding, inspire action, and contribute to creating a culture that values the environment. However, the challenge lies in conveying messages about complex environmental issues in ways that resonate with diverse audiences and incite sustainable behaviors.

NLP Techniques for More Persuasive and Impactful Environmental Communication

NLP offers a wealth of techniques that can enhance the effectiveness of environmental communication:

Reframing: This technique helps change the perception of an event or behavior. For instance, climate change can be reframed from a distant, overwhelming problem to a personal, immediate issue affecting our local communities.

Metaphors and Stories: Stories can simplify complex issues and evoke emotions, making the message more memorable. Metaphors, too, can make abstract concepts tangible. For example, comparing the Earth to a sick patient can help people grasp the urgency of environmental degradation.

Matching and Mirroring: This NLP technique is about adapting one's communication style to that of the listener, facilitating better understanding and rapport. In the context of environmental communication, it could involve using language and examples that resonate with a specific audience.

Anchoring: This involves associating a certain state of mind with a specific stimulus. For instance, images of pristine natural landscapes can be used as anchors to evoke feelings of peace and motivation to protect the environment.

Case Studies: Success Stories of NLP in Environmental Communication

Several organizations and campaigns have successfully leveraged NLP techniques in their environmental communication strategies:

WWF's Earth Hour: The Earth Hour campaign uses anchoring effectively. The act of switching off lights is associated with a commitment to the planet, making it a powerful symbol of environmental responsibility.

Al Gore's "An Inconvenient Truth": The use of storytelling and metaphors in this documentary made the complex issue of climate change accessible and emotionally compelling to a broad audience.

Plastic Pollution Coalition's "Open Your Eyes": This campaign reframed plastic pollution from an abstract issue to a personal health problem, using strong visuals of microplastics in water and food to drive the message home.

In conclusion, the application of NLP techniques in environmental communication can make our messages more persuasive and impactful, thereby promoting sustainable behavior. As environmental communicators, we must continuously refine our skills and techniques to effectively convey the urgency of our planetary predicament and inspire action.

Behavior change, particularly in the context of the environment and sustainability, can be challenging. Multiple barriers often hinder the adoption of sustainable practices. This chapter explores the common obstacles to environmental behavior change, how NLP can help overcome these, and case studies where NLP has successfully mitigated resistance.

Common Obstacles to Environmental Behavior Change

Lack of Awareness or Knowledge: Many individuals lack sufficient understanding of environmental issues, which can hinder their motivation to change behavior.

Perceived Inconvenience or Sacrifice: Often, people perceive sustainable behavior as inconvenient or as requiring significant sacrifices, creating resistance to change.

Belief in the Inefficacy of Individual Action: Some people believe their individual efforts won't make a difference on a global scale, undermining motivation to act sustainably.

Societal Norms and Pressure: Existing societal norms and peer pressure can discourage individuals from adopting practices perceived as 'different' or 'unusual'.

NLP Strategies for Overcoming Resistance to Change

Reframing: NLP's reframing technique can shift perceptions of inconvenience or sacrifice to opportunities for personal benefits, such as health improvements or cost savings.

Metaphors and Storytelling: These techniques can simplify complex environmental issues and highlight the importance and impact of individual actions.

Anchoring Positive Emotions: By associating sustainable actions with positive emotions, NLP can make these behaviors more attractive, reducing resistance.

Future Pacing: This NLP technique helps individuals visualize the positive outcomes of sustainable behaviors, making the future benefits tangible in the present and motivating change.

Case Studies: Examples Where NLP Has Successfully Mitigated Resistance to Change

The "Step it Up!" Campaign: A campaign aimed at promoting walking instead of driving for short distances used NLP techniques to overcome resistance. Reframing walking as an opportunity for exercise and a way to save money helped overcome the perceived inconvenience. Moreover, they used positive anchoring, linking walking to feelings of accomplishment and independence.

The "Meatless Monday" Movement: This global movement faced the challenge of altering deeply ingrained dietary habits. By reframing the concept as an opportunity to explore diverse cuisines and improve health, they helped overcome resistance to change. Also, the narrative of making a difference one day a week made the goal appear achievable and emphasized the impact of collective individual actions.

IKEA's "Live Lagom" Project: IKEA UK ran this project to encourage customers to live a more sustainable life at home. Using future pacing, they highlighted the future benefits of sustainable living, like lower utility bills and a more comfortable home environment. This vision helped reduce resistance to change among participants.

Overcoming barriers to change is crucial in fostering sustainable behaviors. With NLP's strategic approach, we can mitigate resistance and pave the way for environmental behavior change at a broader scale.

While NLP holds great promise in promoting environmental behavior change, it's important to acknowledge the challenges and limitations associated with its application. This chapter discusses ethical considerations, potential constraints, and the future of NLP in environmental behavior change.

Ethical Considerations in Applying NLP for Behavior Change

Manipulation Concerns: Using NLP techniques to influence behavior can raise ethical issues. It's crucial to ensure that such techniques are used transparently and with the consent of the individuals involved, respecting their autonomy and freedom of choice.

Cultural Sensitivity: Environmental issues and sustainable behaviors can be interpreted differently across cultures. NLP practitioners need to be mindful of cultural nuances and adapt their communication to be respectful and effective.

Ensuring Accuracy: In conveying environmental issues, the integrity of information is critical. Practitioners must ensure that NLP techniques, while simplifying complex issues, do not distort or oversimplify the facts.

Potential Limitations and How to Mitigate Them

Effectiveness Varies: NLP's effectiveness can depend on several factors like the individual's personality, their previous experiences, and cultural background. This requires practitioners to be flexible and adaptive in their approach.

Requires Trained Practitioners: Effective use of NLP techniques often requires trained practitioners, which can be a resource constraint for many organizations.

To mitigate these limitations, organizations can invest in NLP training for their staff and develop tailored NLP strategies that consider the unique characteristics of their target audiences.

The Future of NLP in Environmental Behavior Change: Possibilities and Constraints

NLP's potential in environmental behavior change is immense. Its flexible techniques can be tailored to diverse audiences and contexts, making it a valuable tool in environmental communication, education, and advocacy. As we refine our understanding of NLP and its applications, we can expect it to play an even more significant role in promoting sustainable choices.

However, this potential is tempered by certain constraints. The need for trained practitioners, cultural differences, and ethical considerations are among the challenges that must be navigated. Moreover, NLP is just one piece of the puzzle. It should be used alongside other strategies like policy changes, infrastructural improvements, and economic incentives to effectively drive environmental behavior change.

In conclusion, while there are challenges and limitations in applying NLP to environmental behavior change, its potential benefits make it a worthy avenue to explore. By acknowledging and addressing these constraints, we can use NLP effectively and ethically to encourage sustainable choices.

This book has explored the innovative approach of using Neuro-Linguistic Programming (NLP) to foster environmental behavior change and encourage sustainable choices. Now, it's time to recap the key findings and look ahead at the future of this fascinating intersection of psychology and sustainability.

Summary of Key Findings and Insights

We delved into the foundations of NLP, its principles, and techniques, highlighting its potential for shaping perceptions, attitudes, and behaviors. In exploring environmental behavior, we noted various influences, from awareness and knowledge to societal norms and beliefs about the efficacy of individual actions.

The connection between NLP and behavior change was made evident through various case studies, illustrating how reframing, anchoring, and other NLP techniques can encourage sustainable actions. We also saw successful applications of NLP in environmental education and communication, reinforcing its potential as a tool for engagement and impact.

However, we also acknowledged the challenges and ethical considerations in applying NLP, including cultural nuances, the need for trained practitioners, and concerns about manipulation.

Potential Future Applications of NLP in Promoting Sustainability

Looking forward, there's significant potential for expanding the application of NLP in promoting sustainability. Some possibilities include:

Policy Advocacy: NLP techniques could be employed to communicate the need for policy changes more effectively, garnering public support for environmental regulations.

Corporate Sustainability: Businesses could use NLP to encourage sustainable behaviors among employees and to communicate their sustainability efforts to consumers in a more engaging manner.

Climate Change Communication: With climate change being a complex and often polarizing issue, NLP could be used to craft messages that resonate with diverse audiences and motivate collective action.

How This Approach Contributes to the Wider Goal of Environmental Sustainability

As part of a broader toolkit, NLP contributes to environmental sustainability by empowering individuals, organizations, and societies to understand, communicate, and act on environmental issues more effectively. By shaping perceptions and attitudes, fostering engagement, and motivating action, NLP can play a significant role in our collective journey towards a more sustainable world.

As we move forward, it will be important to continuously learn, adapt, and innovate, leveraging tools like NLP to address the pressing environmental challenges of our time. The intersection of psychology and sustainability offers fertile ground for further research and practice, holding the promise of transformative change towards a sustainable future.

Rex Morton is a renowned author and researcher in the United Kingdom with a passionate interest in the human mind, specifically in Cognitive Behavioural Therapy (CBT) and Neuro-Linguistic Programming (NLP).

Morton has spent a considerable portion of his professional life diving deep into the theories and principles that form the backbone of these two compelling fields. His fascination with NLP led him to complete an extensive certification program, solidifying his understanding of this innovative approach to understanding human behaviour.

Although Morton does not have clinical experience, his intense curiosity and dedication to studying these subjects have made him a respected figure in the field. He has thoroughly researched the integration of NLP techniques into CBT, offering fresh perspectives and insights into how these two methodologies can complement each other to enhance understanding of human cognition and behaviour.

As an author, Morton has successfully communicated his knowledge and passion to a broader audience, making complex psychological theories accessible to professionals and interested laypersons. His writing is characterized by a clear, engaging style and a focus on the practical application of theories, making them relevant to everyday life.

In his personal life, Morton is an ardent lover of the natural world, often spending his free time exploring the British countryside. His passion for landscape photography allows him to capture and share the beauty of these excursions. Despite his accomplishments, Morton is known for his humility and eagerness to continue learning. His work continues to inspire those interested in the intricate workings of the human mind and the exciting possibilities presented by the integration of NLP and CBT.

If you've found the content of this book enlightening and wish to continue your journey of understanding the human mind, I warmly invite you to visit my website at www.rexmorton.com. The website serves as a hub of knowledge where I share my latest findings, thoughts, and insights on the integration of NLP and CBT.

I also encourage you to subscribe to the newsletter available on the website. By subscribing, you'll receive regular updates on a range of topics, from detailed discussions on specific NLP techniques and their application in CBT, to the latest research in the field.

The newsletter is also the first place I'll share news of upcoming releases. Whether it's the announcement of a new book, the launch of an online course, newsletter subscribers will be the first to know. This is a great opportunity to continue learning directly from me, deepening your understanding of NLP and CBT, and enhancing your skills in applying these techniques in your own life or professional practice.

I'm looking forward to sharing this journey with you.

As an author, Morton has successfully communicated his knowledge and passion to a broader audience, making complex psychologica theories accessible to professionals and interested laypersons. His writing is characteriz by a clear, engaging style and a focus on the practical application of theories, making them relevant to everyday life.

In this groundbreaking exploration of Neuro-Linguistic Programming (NLP) and environmental behavior change, "Application of Neuro-Linguistic Programming in Environmental Behavior Change: Encouraging Sustainable Choices" serves as a comprehensive guide to promoting sustainability through behavior change.

The book introduces the reader to the rich tapestry o NLP - its history, fundamental principles, and various techniques. It then delves into the multifaceted realm of environmental behavior and what influences it. Th core of the book is devoted to uncovering the links between NLP and behavior change, showcasing through numerous case studies how NLP techniques like reframing, anchoring, and swish pattern can positively influence perceptions about sustainability.

Awakening Your Inner Warrior
Secrets to Unshakeable Confidence
Frank J. Carter